DUE DATE

Jacob and Esau

Series editor: Rachel Cooke
Art director: Jonathan Hair
Consultants: Reverend Richard Adfield; Marlena Schmool
and Samantha Blendis, Board of Deputies of British Jews

First published in 2000 by Franklin Watts

First American edition 2000 by Franklin Watts
A Division of Grolier Publishing
90 Sherman Turnpike
Danbury, CT 06816

Visit Franklin Watts on the Internet at:
http://publishing.grolier.com

Auld, Mary.
    Jacob and Esau/retold by Mary Auld; illustrated by Diana Mayo.--
1st American ed.
        p.cm: -- (Bible stories)
    Summary: Retells the story of the relationship between two
brothers and how one uses trickery to gain their father's blessing
meant for the other.
    ISBN 0-531-14586-7 (library ed.). -- ISBN 0-531-15436-X (pbk.)
    1. Jacob (Biblical patriarch)--Juvenile literature. 2. Esau (Biblical
figure)--Juvenile literature. [1. Jacob (Biblical patriarch). 2. Esau
(Biblical figure) 3. Bible stories--O.T.] I. Mayo, Diana, ill. II. Title.

BS580.J3 A85 2000
222'.1109505--dc21
                                                        99-055974

Jacob and Esau

Retold by Mary Auld

Illustrated by Diana Mayo

W

FRANKLIN WATTS

A Division of Grolier Publishing

NEW YORK • LONDON • HONG KONG • SYDNEY

DANBURY, CONNECTICUT

Long ago in the land of Canaan, Isaac, son of Abraham, married Rebekah. Isaac loved his wife, but they were both sad because they had no children. Isaac prayed to God to give Rebekah a child.

God answered Isaac's prayer and Rebekah became pregnant. But there seemed to be a constant struggle inside her womb. Rebekah asked God what was happening to her.

"There are two nations in your womb," replied God. "Two separate peoples shall come out of your body. One people shall be stronger than the other; and the older will serve the younger."

And when the time came for
Rebekah to give birth, she had twins.

The first twin to come out was red,
and covered in hair, so they named
him Esau. The second followed swiftly
after, grasping his brother by the heel.
Rebekah and Isaac called him Jacob.

The boys grew up. Esau became
a skillful hunter, an outdoorsman.
Jacob was quiet and stayed at home,
keeping close to the tents. Isaac loved
Esau, because he liked to eat the
animals Esau caught while hunting,
but Rebekah loved Jacob.

One day, Jacob was cooking a stew when Esau returned from hunting, ravenously hungry. "Give me some of that red stuff," Esau begged Jacob. "I'm famished!"

"Only if you sell me your birthright," replied Jacob, "so that I will have the right of the firstborn son, not you."

"I'm about to starve to death," said Esau. "What good is a birthright to me?"

"Swear to it first," said Jacob.

So Esau swore an oath, selling his birthright to Jacob, and ate his fill of the red stew. He gave up his birthright without a second thought.

Time passed. Isaac grew old, and his
eyesight dimmed so that he could no
longer see. He called Esau to him. "My
son," he said. "I am now an old man
and may soon die. Take your bow and

10

arrow and go out and hunt some
animals for me. Use them to make me
one of those tasty meals that I love so
much. Then I can give you my blessing
before I die." So Esau set out on his hunt.

 11

Rebekah had been listening when Isaac spoke to Esau. She found Jacob, her favorite son, and told him all she had heard. Then she said: "Listen carefully, and do just what I tell you. Go out to the flock and bring me two choice kids, and I will make a meal for your father, just the way he likes it. Then you can take it to him and receive his blessing instead of Esau."

"But Esau is hairy, and my skin is smooth," worried Jacob. "What if my father touches me? He will think I am tricking him and curse me rather than bless me."

"The curse will be on me!" his mother replied. "Just do what I say and fetch those goats."

Jacob did as his mother told him. He brought her the kids, and she prepared his father's favorite dish. Then Rebekah took Esau's best clothes and made Jacob dress in them. She also covered Jacob's hands and neck with the hairy skin of the kids. Finally, she placed the dish of food in Jacob's hands and sent him off to his father.

Isaac heard Jacob arriving. "Who is it?" he asked.

"It is Esau, your firstborn," lied Jacob. "I have done as you told me. Please sit up and eat this meat so that I can receive your blessing."

"How did you find the meat so quickly?" asked Isaac.

"God gave me success," explained Jacob.

Isaac asked his son to come closer and touched his skin. "Your voice is Jacob's voice, but your hands are Esau's," he said. "Are you really my son Esau?"

"I am," said Jacob.

So Isaac ate the meal, and then

kissed his son. As he did so, he smelled Esau's clothes on Jacob. "Ah, the smell of my son is like the smell of the fields that God has blessed," Isaac exclaimed, and he blessed Jacob, saying, "May God give you riches from heaven and earth. Let peoples serve you and nations bow down to you. Be lord over your brothers. Cursed are those that curse you and blessed are those who bless you."

No sooner had Isaac finished his
blessing and Jacob left than Esau
returned from hunting. He prepared the
meal and went to Isaac. "Please sit up,
my father," he said, "and eat this meat
so that I can receive your blessing."

"Who are you?" demanded Isaac.

"I am Esau, your firstborn son,"
replied Esau.

Isaac began to tremble violently.
"Who was it who brought me a meal
just now?" he asked. "I blessed him —
and he will remain blessed! Your
brother has taken your blessing."

"Jacob has already taken my birthright, and now he has my blessing. Have you no blessing for me?" Esau asked Isaac.

"I have made Jacob lord over you and given him riches," his father replied. "What can I possibly give you?"

"Have you only one blessing? Bless me too, Father!" begged Esau. And he broke into loud sobs.

So Isaac blessed Esau. "You will live by the sword and you will serve your brother. But when you grow restless, you will break his yoke from your neck."

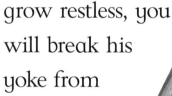

Now Esau held a grudge against Jacob. "After my father dies, I shall kill Jacob," he said to himself. But Rebekah heard of his plans. She went to Jacob and told him to leave. "Go to my brother Laban," she urged him. "Stay with him until Esau is no longer angry and has forgotten what you've done."

Afterwards, Rebekah spoke to Isaac and persuaded him to let Jacob go to Laban, who lived far way in the city of Haran. Isaac agreed and called Jacob to him and told him to leave.

"Marry one of Laban's daughters," Isaac commanded. Then he added,

"May God Almighty bless you and make your family grow so that you become a great people. May He give you and your children the blessing He gave Abraham so that you will have this land, the land He gave to Abraham."

And Jacob set out for his uncle's home.

Before the sun had set, Jacob stopped for the night. With a stone for his pillow, he lay down and slept. And he dreamed of a stairway that stretched from the earth to heaven with the angels of God walking up and down it. God stood above the stairway and spoke to Jacob: "I am the Lord, the God of Abraham and Isaac. I give the land on which you lie to you and your children. Your family will be like the dust of the earth and spread out in all directions and bring blessing to all its people. Remember, I am with you and will protect you wherever you go. I shall bring you back to this land."

Jacob awoke amazed. Using his stone pillow, he built a pillar and poured oil on it, and continued on his way. Later, he called the place Bethel, the house of God.

Jacob lived with his uncle Laban for twenty years. He did well. He married both of Laban's daughters, Leah and Rachel, and, with them and their two maids, he had twelve sons and a daughter. But one day God told him it was time to go back to Canaan.

With all his new family, his servants and flocks of goats, sheep, donkeys, and camels, Jacob set out for home.

Jacob was frightened of meeting
Esau. He realized now the wrong he
had done him, and he sent his servants
ahead with gifts of many animals. But
he need not have worried: Esau greeted
his brother with joy, embracing him
and weeping. Jacob wept, too. Both
brothers knew that God had chosen
Jacob and his children to have the land
of Canaan. Jacob had come home.

About This Story

Jacob and Esau is a retelling of part of Genesis, the first book of the Bible. The Bible is the name given to the collection of writings that are sacred, in different forms, to the Jewish and Christian religions. Genesis, which means "beginning," is the first of 39 books in the Hebrew Bible, Tanakh, or Christian Old Testament. Genesis is also part of the Torah, the first five books of the Bible and the most sacred text of the Jewish religion.

Family Trees

Genesis tells how the relationship between God and His people began. It tells how God chose Abraham and gave him the land of Canaan. God promised it would belong to Abraham's family forever. In return, Abraham promised to live a good and just life, following the ways of God.

Abraham had only one son, Isaac, so the land passed to him. The birth of Esau (whose name means "hairy") and Jacob (meaning "he grasps by the heel") ensured the family line continued, but which son would inherit? Esau, or as he is sometimes called, Edom, was expected to inherit by the birthright of the firstborn son. But Jacob bought his brother's birthright and it is clear Esau did not really understand its value. The birthright is not just land but is God's gift to Abraham and Isaac. Because of this, it is not only the birthright that is important but also Isaac's blessing. Jacob lied to his father to ensure his family, not Esau's, was chosen by God.

Two Nations

The story of Jacob and Esau could almost be a family "soap opera." But their story is really about the beginnings of two nations or peoples, the Israelites and the Edomites. Jacob's descendants were the Israelites (or Hebrews), Esau's the Edomites. The Bible tells how the Israelites were God's

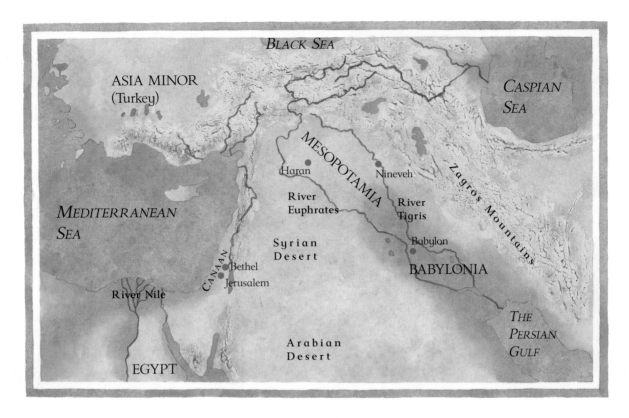

chosen people, the final inheritors of God's promised land, which they called Israel after Jacob (see below). The Israelites explained why their neighbors, the Edomites, spoke a similar language by connecting them to Esau.

The Patriarchs

The Jewish religion, and later Christianity, began among the Israelites, which is why their story is so important. The Israelites called Abraham, Isaac, and Jacob the Patriarchs, or fathers, while Jacob's sons and two of his grandsons gave their names to the twelve tribes of Israel.

The Patriarchs are not perfect. Jacob in particular is very human – he lies to his father and knows just how to get around his brother. But after his dream at Bethel, he listens to God and is aware of His greatness. On his return to Canaan, Jacob is renamed Israel by God. Israel means "to strive to understand God," suggesting a challenge that Jacob shares with all his descendants.

29

Useful Words

Angels Angels are messengers from God.

Birthright People's birthright is what they receive because of their position in the family. In the past, the birthright of a family's eldest son meant that he usually inherited most of his parents' land and wealth.

Blessing A blessing is a way of wishing someone happiness and success in the future. Blessings are often thought to be gifts from God. Isaac's blessings passed to his sons not only his wishes for their future but also those of God.

Canaan Canaan is an ancient name for a region of the Middle East which now makes up most of modern day Israel, Palestine, and part of Lebanon (see map on page 29).

Curse To curse is to wish someone unhappiness and disaster in the future.

Grudge A grudge is an angry feeling that people have about someone who they think has done something wrong to them in the past.

Nation In this story, a nation is a large group of people who share the same ancestors, language, lifestyle, and beliefs. A nation can also mean a country or state with its own laws and government.

Oath An oath is a very strong promise, which people swear on something very important, such as their religious beliefs, as a kind of guarantee. If they break the oath, they also betray their beliefs.

Pray When people pray they talk to God, to worship Him, to ask Him for help, and to feel close to Him. Some prayers are said out loud in a group. Others are said on your own, quietly or in your head.

Womb The womb is the part of a woman's body in which babies grow until they are born.

Yoke A yoke is the heavy wooden frame that joins two oxen (a type of cow) together across the shoulder so that they can pull heavy farm machinery, such as a plow. People often describe the hard work of being a slave or servant as a yoke.

What Do You Think?

These are some questions about *Jacob and Esau* to ask yourself and to talk about with other people.

How do you think Rebekah felt about being pregnant?

Who would you prefer, Jacob or Esau? Why?

What did you think of Esau when he sold his birthright?

How do you think Rebekah influenced Jacob?

What do you think Jacob felt when he lied to his father?

Why do you think Isaac's blessing is so important?

How would you feel if your brother stole something from you?

What do you think Jacob's dream at Bethel meant?

How would you feel if you returned home after many years away?